Dear Sir

a

professional scribe

shows how to lay out handwritten

letters

and

envelopes

so that they are fun to write

and

interesting

to

read

GU00707648

By the same Author

❖

❖

Dear Sir

how
to make your
handwritten letters
works of
art

by

George L. Thomson

Thorsons Publishers
Limited
Wellingborough
Northamptonshire

First
published
1·9·8·4

© George L. Thomson
1984

British Library Cataloguing in Publication Data

Thomson, George L.
Dear Sir
1. Letter-writing
1. Title
808·6   PE1483

ISBN 0-7225-0949-9

Printed and bound in Great Britain

Many of the decorations in this book are rubber stamps, used in the same way as an office date stamp, with an ink pad. They are hand made from ordinary pencil erasers, and the white parts are cut away as in linocuts, wood engravings or potato cuts, using a sharp cutting tool. The whole process is described in detail in "Rubber Stamps — how to make them," along with examples and suggestions for many and varied uses, such as making greetings cards, decorative wrapping papers and hand printed posters.

Contents

❖

1 Variations on a Theme

1579 Jacaranda Drive, San Leandro, CA 81112
2nd November, 1981

Dear Sir,

There was a time when handwriting was taught in schools as a regular subject, like geography, history and English. Most people could write fairly well when they left school, simply because they were required to practice regularly.

Now the results of dropping Handwriting from the curriculum are plain to see. A reasonably nicely written letter is now a matter for comment, instead of an everyday occurrence. Yours

G Bickham

N.L.B. VIII

top of page

3 Lancaster Road · SW8   22 December, 1989

Dear Robert —

Thank you for your letter and kind comments. I
  agree — LETTERS NEED NOT BE DULL! You may not
  be able to write like this, but if you use your normal
  handwriting, taking just enough extra time to write
  legibly, and follow the letter layouts I suggest,
  then your letters will immediately look better.

If you are then inspired to go further, you will have
  the incentive to spend a little MORE time in acquiring
  a basic Italic hand.

Even routine, humdrum matters can be written to LOOK
  interesting, well worth the little extra effort required.
  You may say you can't spare the time. Try timing
  yourself on a scribbled letter, and the same one written
  reasonably carefully. You will agree the extra few
  minutes are time well spent.   Yours —

Irene

top of page

240 Barr Boulevard

North Vancouver · B·C·

Telephone   251·36·8924

November 2, 1982

Dear Owen -

It has often been pointed out to me that any interest in handwriting
is just so much wasted effort, because in a few years time
we'll all be using wrist communicators. Then grammar
and spelling, as well as reading and writing, will become
extinct.

Maybe -! With the invention of the automobile, it was confidently
predicted that the horse would soon be a rarity. I now read
that in Britain at least, there are MORE horses than
there were in 1920.

Again, when I was a young teacher in 1949, I was seriously advised
to forget italic handwriting, because within twenty years
everyone, child or adult, would own a typewriter. Even now,
this seems improbable. And more and more people are
quite perversely actually taking PLEASURE in writing by hand!

Theophilus

top of page

1729 Carrier Avenue
ASHEVILLE · NC·28971

Telephone · 524·619·13

28 March · 1982

Dear Mae — Here is a list of the books you wanted. First, the ones about Italic Handwriting.

✦

Cursive Handwriting	Philip A. Burgoyne	Dryad
A Handwriting Manual	Alfred Fairbank	Faber · Pentalic
Italic Handwriting	Tom Gourdie	Studio · Pentalic
The New Better Handwriting	George L Thomson	Canongate · Pentalic · Douglas & McIntyre
Omnibus Copy Book	Irene Wellington	Allen & Unwin

✦

Formal Writing —

Writing & Illuminating & Lettering	Edward Johnston	Pitman · Pentalic
The Calligrapher's Handbook	C. M. Lamb [Ed.]	Faber · Pentalic

✦

About rubber stamps (1) and how to make your own (2)

(1) The Rubber Stamp Album	Miller & Thompson	Workman Publishing
(2) Rubber Stamps and Seals	George L Thomson	Canongate · Pentalic

✦

Yours sincerely — Frank

16

top of page

2 Heath Lane, LONDON   Telephone 01·323·5920

3 September 1986

Dear Ted

You asked if there was any way to add variety
   to your writing without going to the trouble
   of using different size pens.
This is probably the simplest way - all you need
   do is make your writing larger, using the same
   pen.
But be sure to give plenty of margin space. when
   the lines of writing are as close as this, the
   margins MUST be generous to prevent a cramped
   appearance.
with lines as close as this, too, there can be problems
   with the tangling of ascenders & descenders.

yours - Derek

top of page

The Firs, Ann Road, Bath **bg** 14 January, 1 9 8 4

Dear Wendy – when you use different sizes of pens, it is possible to make a very lively letter layout, but note that more than three sizes can make for a fussy appearance, unless very well planned.

Paragraphs may be shown in various ways – by indenting the beginning word, as in type; or better, starting outside the left margin, as here, which is how most scribes did it before the printing press. Also, as here, a line can be missed between paragraphs.

A decorative heading may be made from the writer's initials, as I have shown above. These can be quite plainly written, or a more decorative style may be used. — Yours –

Bill Giles

20

top of page

Wednesday   5 May 1991

The White Cottage · Balgrie Bank · Bonnybank · by LEVEN · KY8·5SL

Dear Beki -

As you say, everyone likes to receive a beautifully hand-written letter. The most perfectly typed letter always looks cold and impersonal in comparison.

In a pile of mail, the envelopes which are NOTICED are the hand written ones, provided they are legible, and it can be seen that some minimal care has been taken in setting out the address. The same applies to the letter inside – LEGIBILITY must come first, then presentation.

Typing MAY be faster, [not always, if you are a two-finger operator], but a very little extra time spent on writing what you have to say in a pleasant way will pay dividends.

The recipient will derive pleasure from the mere appearance of your letter, no matter how dull the contents may be.

Yours -

George

top of page

Dear Penelope

What sort of pens do I recommend? Use the pens you can
    afford. They come in many prices – the higher the
    price, the more esteemed as a status symbol. But a
    pen made from 22 carat gold, studded with diamonds,
    does not ensure you will write any better than with a
    cheap plastic one bought in your local store.

The difference in performance is minimal. You might very
    well find that an "old-fashioned" dip pen does perfectly
    for YOU, rather than a fountain pen. Or you may still
    prefer a ballpoint or fibre tip.

This is written with an old Osmiroid 75, fitted with a fine
    italic nib. The larger writing is done with a Platignum
    pen with a medium nib. I also use a Pelikan 120,
    also with a fine italic nib.   Yours –

Raymond

top of page

21 May 1982   01·982·3084

Oak Cottage · Lee Lane West · Whitley Village · Shirehampton, Leeds

Dear Andrew

Even if you only use one size of pen, your letters will look attractive if you lay them out like this, with plenty of margin space all round. Different pen sizes will give more contrast.

Here I have used a decorative crest. In this case it is a hand cut rubber stamp, but it can be a line block or wood engraving. The design can be chosen for its significance to the writer, or simply for decoration.

Yours
Jonathan

top of page

29 Wrotham Gardens,
Filton, Abingdon,
Berkshire · 0176 · 31728

15th November, 1987

Dear Maisie — When one has to pack a great deal of information into a limited space, how, do you ask, does one preserve the attractive appearance of the page? ⊙ One way is to run the writing right to the end of each line, marking the paragraphs in some way. ⊙ Here I am using a very small rubber stamp. This particular one is very simple, but more decorative ones may be used. ⊙ An asterisk can be usefully employed in this sort of situation. ⊙ Before the invention of the printing press, scribes used this mark at the beginning of a paragraph ¶, and printers adopted it and may still use it. ⊙ Though it is permissible to use less generous margins than usual, it is wise to leave as much space as possible round the edges of the page. ⊙ As with any other letter, leave the biggest space at the foot of the page. If the writing continues nearly to the bottom, the page will have a "heavy" appearance. ⊙ This sort of arrangement is very useful in writing air mail letters, where the writing of an extra page may cost you an extra stamp. ⊙   Yours —

Stanley

top of page

Parchment Farm · Waterfoot · Southfield · Hants GA3·3EB
12·6·1984

Dear William

As you have noticed, I like to use rubber stamp decorations on
my letters – and envelopes. It is better, I feel, to have a box
full of stamps, and to be able to change the heading at will.
In the past I have had headings printed on my stationery, but
long before the box is finished I have tired of the design.
This way I have freedom to change the print on every letter I
write if I feel like it. It is much more fun to use a variety
of prints.
These rubber stamps can be bought, but it is much cheaper, more
enjoyable and more satisfying to make your own. There is
a book by George L Thomson which shows you how.
Many years ago I used to add drawings to illustrate my letters,
but this I have to agree is time-consuming!   Yours–

Dorothy

30

top of page

Friday · 3 August · 1981   Telephone : 091 · 362 · 5411

4 King's Court · Whitley · Leeds · LP 923 · 6 RE

Dear Marie

(Proper layout and spacing will improve any letter. FIRST – give your text "room to breathe". Most people use up all the available space, writing up to the very edge of the paper. Never do this. SECOND : make sure your address, date, & telephone number are legible and well placed.

(The text of the letter should be easily read ; apart from simple legibility, the paragraphs should be easily seen, and the beginnings marked in some way. The first letter or word can for instance be a larger pen size or a different colour. (Experiment with different methods .

Yours –

Frederick B.

top of page

36 White Horse Close ⁑ Southsea ⁑ Redhill ⁑ Cornwall ⁑ D15·1AB
18th January · 1988

Dear Heather

With more space between the lines, it is possible to
use much longer ascenders and descenders,
and as you can see, a most elegant effect
can be obtained. This kind of letter
is useful for invitations and letters of
thanks and other events of a more ceremonial
nature. Avoid "fancy" ascenders and descenders-
try to keep them as simple as these. Yours-

Jennifer

top of page

The Shieling · Ardcraig · Rannoch · Argyll · Scotland · 27 December '83

Dear Mary Rae

Should you already have a passable written script, it is possible to
    vary it by compression, as here, as well as by changing
    the height of the letters as has already been suggested,
    or by using either larger or smaller pens.

With a typewriter, one is limited to only one script, with
    its small letters and capitals, and it is difficult to avoid
    monotony.

Using one or two extra pens, it is a simple matter to
    change size to make an ACCENT, instead of underlining
    the word.   yours-

(Tom

top of page

3106 Main Street, Gretna,
LOUISIANA · 80253 · U·S·A

24 July · 1 9 9 4
Phone: [534] 432 3279

Dear Judy —

There is no doubt that a well laid out and nicely written letter
will catch the eye of a prospective employer before even
the neatest of typewritten letters. When I was 15, I applied
for a job, and was one of only six chosen for an interview
out of nearly 100 applicants. [I used ordinary handwriting —
I had not heard of italic then.]

Some years ago a student to whom I had taught italic was chosen
against similar odds, and got the job even though some of
the others were better qualified. His employers told him
it was his letter which decided the vote in his favour.

Try to keep your letter of application short and simple. State
your qualifications and why you want to work for this
organization. Try to keep it on one page — fuller details
can be supplied on an extra sheet if necessary.

yours —

Simon

top of page

Ardshiel · High Ley · Ipswich  Telephone : 096 · 33 · 5412

24 June 1983

Dear James Barr

You will have noticed that I prefer the symmetrically
balanced letter layout. This is easily achieved
if you use a ruled underlay sheet which goes
under your writing paper. (Most writing paper
is thin enough so that the black ruled lines will
show through.) Add a vertical line down the
centre, and one or two more as guides for the
side margins.

As a decorative heading I have here written a Gothic
or Black Letter "G". Anyone who is insufficiently
skilled to write an initial could buy (or make)
a rubber stamp for the desired letter.   Yours—

Frances Goldenring

top of page

7392 Las Vegas Boulevard · La Jolla · California · 9 3 7 2 0
14 July 1981

Dear Norman

Better buy rubber stamps to make special initial letters, if you don't have enough confidence yet to make them with your pen. Keep practising anyway!

Lots of firms supply stamps in U.S.A, few in U.K. The general standard of art work is poor, but shop around for a good catalog — there ARE some.

Original rubber stamp designs by George L Thomson can be got from B.M.Blue, 5089 Pasadena Avenue, Sacramento, CA·95841, also any of his books. There is one on how to make your own rubber stamps which should interest you.

Yours —

Robin

top of page

144 West Gate · Centerville · West Chester · Telephone [432] 316 7145
15 December 1993

Before you give up, Jean, on the grounds that you can't afford to buy fancy pens, consider this. The "B" you see here was written with a handmade bamboo pen. Bamboo is hollow-stemmed, and any woody and hollow-stemmed plant will serve to make a pen.

Similarly, you can pick up a feather and make yourself a free but perfectly serviceable pen. This is written with a goose quill which I have just cut. The first paragraph is written with a fountain pen for comparison.

If you keep geese-or turkeys-fine; but town dwellers may pick up feathers in a park or zoo. Any feather will serve, peacock, goose, pelican – whatever. Duck, chicken or crow will make very fine-pointed pens. Practice on larger ones to begin with. Any good book on formal lettering will show you how to cut bamboo and quill pens.   Yours-

Bernard

top of page

The Crafts Arcade
1426 Belle Avenue · Hardifield
STONYFORD
6·14·87

Dear Kristin

Since you are not keen on the more illustrative designs for your
notepaper, may I suggest something like this? Using a set
of rubber stamps, you can build up an almost infinite series
of designs like this. If you make one you particularly like,
your local printer can reproduce it for you, so that you can
have it on all your notepaper.   But though you will save
time, you will miss the fun of inventing a new design
for every letter!
Yours -

Hayes J.

top of page

Willow Grove House · Mill Street · Maidstone
KENT
26 March '88

Dear Gerald

Here is an example of a letter using a formal layout and

a more formal italic script. This MUST of course

take more time than an ordinary letter, and you

yourself must decide whether the occasion justifies

the extra care required. On the other hand, the

effect you get this way may be sufficient recompense

no matter what the actual content of the letter.

Yours-

Millicent

top of page

Badbea · Elm Way · BOSTON   9 January · 1 9 8 7

Dear Elizabeth – You wanted to know how many ways a letter can be arranged. It would seem there is no end to the possibilities.

Obviously you must have your own address, with the date, and telephone number if you have one. Only convention says this information must be at the beginning of a letter. It could just as well be at the end.

When writing to an old friend who knows your address as well as his own, it is feasible to miss out the information entirely. This opens the possibility of a more decorative beginning to your letter.

Yours –

Stuart

top of page

Oakwood · Camden Lane · Tidworth · Herts · AL5 · OJP · 30 April '83

Dear Graham

The prime rule in writing is to aim for legibility. To convey your thought to others, your writing MUST be decipherable. Using an illegible scribble is an insult to the recipient, as much as talking at the dinner table with your mouth full.

Signatures also should be readable, but too many people seem to think a dashing scribble shows "character." I suspect they feel the less legible, the higher their status.

Like the illiterate kings and dignitaries of past ages, they have to hire and pay scribes [typists] to write their letters, to which they add a seal, a thumbprint — or a squiggle — to authenticate it!

Some claim it saves time to sign with a squiggle; and some super-timesavers even have a rubber stamp made of their squiggle so as to save more time still. No doubt they then use the time to watch steel balls bouncing at the end of strings!

yours -
Therese

top of page

Ardstiel
Heath Place
Newquay

15 August 1987

064·99·5632

Dear Kenneth

Why are letters always upright, you ask? They need not be.
This page could be just as attractive turned on its side.
Or the page could be square, or long and narrow.
[Sometimes one can acquire stationer's offcuts in odd sizes.]

The distinguished bookbinder, Anthony Gardner's letters are
unusual for being written in a spiral. For everyday
use this might be a bit tedious to write out — or read —
but for special occasions it can be highly effective.

Use any form you can devise, bearing in mind that it should
be possible to read through the letter from beginning to
end without ambiguous jumps from place to place.

Yours -

Alicia May

top of page

Spruce Farm · Redhill · Bambury · Kent · 0721·710621

14 June 1983

Dear Nancy · No, if you use a decorative motif on your letters, it doesn't HAVE to be in the centre of the page.

An assymmetrical arrangement like this can also be quite attractive. But be sure, as always, that you leave sufficient margin space all round, with the widest space at the bottom.

It is sometimes quite advantageous to have plenty of marginal space. Occasionally one may have an afterthought or qualification to what has already been said. This may be comfortably added in the ample margins. Sometimes a contrasting colour may be used.

yours –

Charles

top of page

Crossways · Ash Grove · Pontypool · Gwent
6th February 1985

Dear Joan – It seems you are worried about
how to "square up" the side margins of
your letters.
The left hand one presents no problems – each
word starts immediately below the one
above, so you automatically get a straight
line.
But how does one avoid a ragged line on
the right hand margin? The answer
is, one doesn't! Only when a line of
type is justified does this unnatural
straight line manifest itself.
Avoid splitting up or hyphenating words at
the end of a line if you can. Carry a
long word into the clear space, or stop
short and start the word in the next line.

Bernhard

top of page

THE FIRS

Tudor Avenue · West Maybury · Birmingham · B2 9HX
4 January 1991

Dear Jacques –

It is quite possible to use rubber stamp letters to make
letter headings, as above, depending on the size.
A heading with more letters would need smaller
stamps.

Some immensely patient people write whole letters or
even books, stamping one letter at a time, but
this is not a process I would recommend!

If you buy a set, I advise you to get SIMPLE letters,
which adapt for many purposes, rather than
fanciful or grotesque alphabets made from
animals, twigs, balloons & so on, which very
soon lose any appeal they may have at first. Yours –

Annette

top of page

3412 Lincoln Way

Jamesville · VA 39725

8 15 92

Dear Rhoda

Your letter with beautifully illuminated "D" for Dear arrived this morning. But though I truly do appreciate all the work you put into it, I don't think this is justifiable on an ordinary letter. You could be using the time spent on this much more profitably!

For some very special letter of congratulation, for a wedding or christening, say, THEN all the loving effort may be worthwhile.

Normally a letter will look better if the decoration is kept very simple, and it will also be more readable. Keep the gold and silver and pretty colours for a BOOK that is going to be kept and cherished.   yours —

Edward

top of page

4162 Wilford, Miller Grove, Durban, South Africa
14 · XII · 89

Dear Tim —

What kinds of black ink do I recommend? A
lot depends on where you live, and what is
available in your particular area.

The ones I have used and find quite satisfactory
are Pelikan Fount India, Parker Black
Quink, and Faber-Castell Higgins Eternal
Ink, which is what I am using here.

Some inks are not so dense as others, and some
flow better. Shop around until you find one
that you feel happy with!

Alice

top of page

2358 Thirtysecond Avenue North · Jacksonville · Florida

Monday   2 July 1988

Dear Lawrence

To make it easy to write a balanced letter like this, use the guide on the next page, which you place behind the page you are writing on. Most writing papers are thin enough for you to see the lines faintly shining through. I have supplied some blank sheets of note paper so you can try out this method.

Place THIS letter on top of the template, and you will see how I have used the guide. You may prefer to draw a guide for your own use, with wider or narrower spacing, or different margins. Just be sure to make the lines dark enough.

Yours –

Jacqueline D.

top of page

14·VI·85   *Arden House Newport ·ND·*

Dear Andrew· Apologies for not writing sooner!
Of course I'll be delighted to see you again. I'll meet
you at the airport next Wednesday
You are welcome to stay as long as you like this time,
and I understand you do not have to rush off
somewhere else.

Our swimming pool has been mended, and the kids
look forward to showing you how much they have
progressed since you gave them lessons!

Phone if you think there has to be any change
in the arrangements. Yours affectionately,

Wilma

top of page

2090 Bath Road,
Vancouver, B.C.

12 September,
1981

Dear William,

When you claimed I could improve the look of my
letters simply by changing the layout and by
taking just a little more time on my writing, I
couldn't believe you.

Maybe I have been rushing my letters too much. Now
I shall take an extra minute or so on each one
and see whether I can make any improvement.

Like most people, I suppose, I have not consciously
practised writing at all since I left school. No
wonder letter writing has become a lost art!
Yours,

Sandra

top of page

5264 Wood Lane,
Roseville, CA 96271

Saturday
5 March, 1979

DEAR CRAIG –

Do I object to letters being written with fibre tip or ball point pens? No; if you have always used this type of pen, and do not feel happy with the square cut nib used for italic writing, by all means carry on as you have been doing.

(Perhaps I SHOULD point out that anything written with these pens tends to smudge and blur after a time, so if you want your writing to last [as in a diary, for instance] you would be much better to use ink.

Yours –

Ellery King

top of page

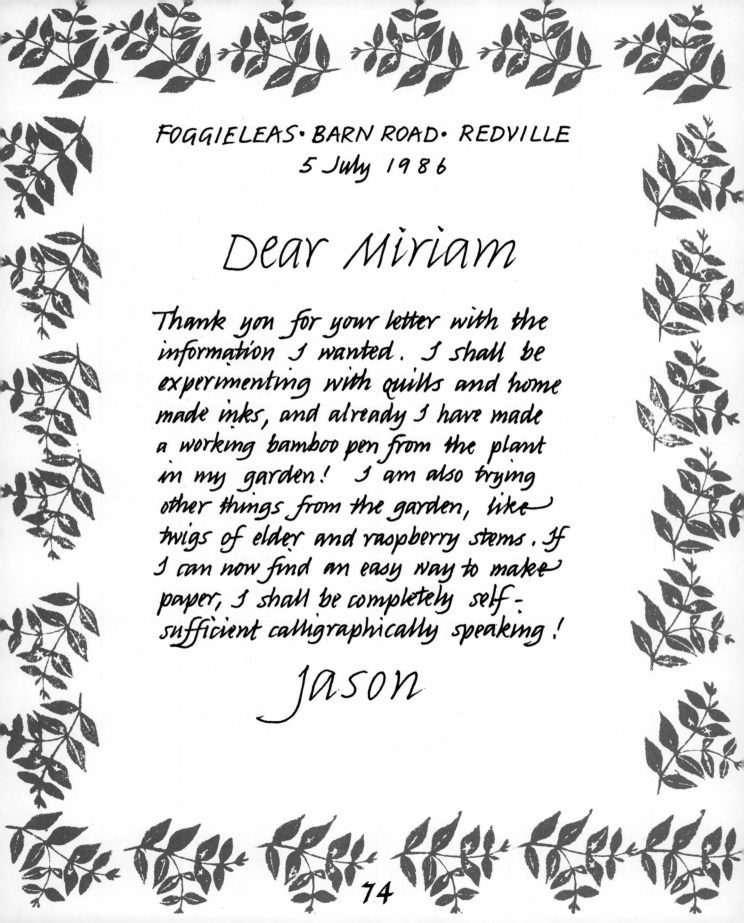

FOGGIELEAS · BARN ROAD · REDVILLE
5 July 1986

Dear Miriam

Thank you for your letter with the
information I wanted. I shall be
experimenting with quills and home
made inks, and already I have made
a working bamboo pen from the plant
in my garden! I am also trying
other things from the garden, like
twigs of elder and raspberry stems. If
I can now find an easy way to make
paper, I shall be completely self-
sufficient calligraphically speaking!

Jason

top of page

324 High St, BANKS   14th July, 1984

Dear Alexander-

Yes, it is quite effective to use a different colour for
    capital letters or the beginning word of a
    paragraph.
The BEST colour to use with black ink is red.
    Blue will make the writing look "cold", and
    green or purple will tend to look affected.
Red has been used as the most suitable colour since
    the earliest days. The ancient Egyptian
    scribes are depicted with palettes containing
    both red and black pigments.
This use of colour can also be employed when
    writing with ballpoint or fibre tip pens,
    when it is actually easier to swap colours. Yours-

Helena

top of page

2 Unusual Layouts

8425 Alamanda Way · San Francisco · California 39214
29 September 1986

Dear Alicia May -

Is this the sort of letter layout you had in mind in your last letter to me?

I have been experimenting with different sizes of pen and varying shapes of paper, and I agree there is a lot of fun doing this, especially for the first time!

When you can spare the time, I would greatly appreciate your comments on this humble effort.

Yours - Kenneth

top of page

Mill House, Toll Road, Bradbury, 15th September, 1981

DEAR

M arcus, For a long time the handwriting taught in most
schools, here and in the United States, has been based on copper-
plate script. When it is written with great care and attention,
using a flexible pointed pen, it can look just passable. When
written by a master penman it can appear impressive, but when
it is done by you and me it looks like nothing very much. At
its best it still looks as if it had been written by a schoolboy.

It is a style which is insipid and characterless without the saving
contrast of thick and thin strokes. And really, most of the copper-
plate writing you see in advertisements is not written anyway — it
is drawn. The thick lines are really two, filled in solid afterwards.
But even this child's writing looks better for being "placed" on the paper! Yours —

Vere Foster

82

top of page

Dear Papa. This is an example of a spirally written letter. (Try a special occasion; this form is JUST acceptable; but mainly, I think this extreme in design should be just for fun! I remember many years ago writing out a spiral PATERNOSTER in versals, and considering, Not long after this, I came across a book with an illustration of an ancient clay tablet of the Phoenicians, Feshtu Gunzporung, humans of years B.C. – and it was written in a spiral! an innovative genius. About the same time I found that Anthony Gardner, the well known bookbinder, had been writing spiral letters for years. It is not easy to have an original idea! Still, I DID think up the idea on my own, made it out of nothing, so to speak. Anyway, if you want to write in a spiral, certainly try it! Yours – Frederick C. Wellington. 15th November, MCMLXIII

84

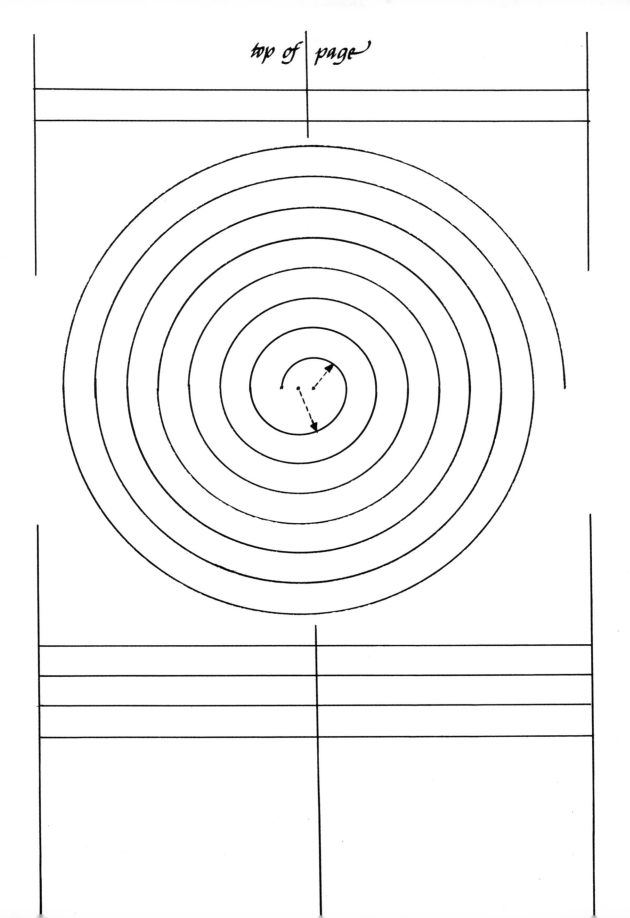

top of page

3 Envelopes

Desmond O'Neill · President · The Astrological Society of Great Britain

Red Lion Lane · Bishop's Court ·

London EC4 · Q12

Glenfinnan Scotland

Hazel Whittaker · 932A Friedrichstrasse W.

Am Weissbaden ³

West Germany

Philip Mazzei
Patriot Remembered

USAirmail
40c

James M Matthewson   DIRECTOR

Griffin Centre of Arts and Crafts

Red Lion Close

London

Mr and Mrs Benbow

14a Whittaker's Alley

ROCKHAMPTON KENT

The Director · Publicity Department · The Arts in Maine

Carnegie Centre · York Avenue · **Artington**

Maria Llano

9832 Morrison Street · First Avenue South

OR· 92765

Portland

Christmas USA 15c

Stacy Morton · 62645 Erickson Road ·

Bend

OREGON·97701

U·S·A

Sandy Lockhart
10 Hatton Court   N·IRELAND

❖ N·IRELAND ❖

Strabane

Andrew Hoffman · Records Branch · City Library

Los Angeles

CA · 729514

Philip (Price) · 4500 Kennedy Avenue

New York NY 37821

top of page

top of page

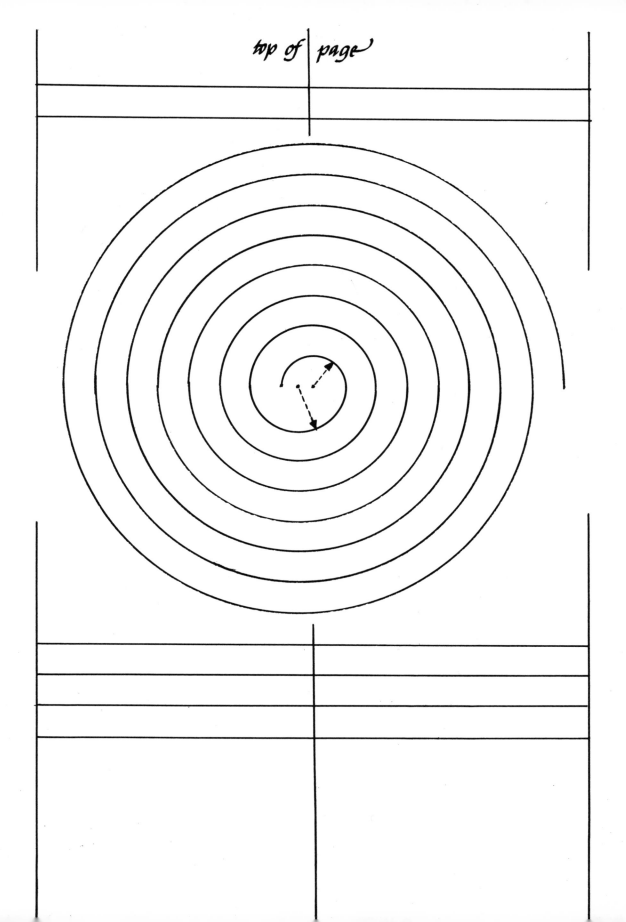

top of page